heavenly bodies

Crab Orchard Series in Poetry
Editor's Selection

Acknowledgments

Grateful acknowledgment is made to the editors of the following magazines and anthologies where these poems (sometimes in earlier versions) originally appeared:

Anti-: "Gher the Hound"

The Best American Erotic Poems from 1800 to the Present, edited by David Lehman: section 4 of "Shot Up in the Sexual Revolution"

The Crab Orchard Review: "Monica"

Crying Sky: "The Elderberries" (originally published as "Blackberry")

The Massachusetts Review: "Cut Flowers"

The New Hampshire Review: "Bride of the Barbiturate" (including versions of "Wake," "Bride of the Barbiturate," and "Recovery Room")

No Tell Motel: "Shot Up in the Sexual Revolution"

TriQuarterly: "Bastard's Song," "Delinquent"

The Wire: "Coyote"

"Dirt Cowboy Café" was presented as the Phi Beta Kappa poem at Dartmouth College in May 2006. "The Elderberries" (originally published as "Blackberry") was featured on *Verse Daily*.

I

Bastard's Song

Your father was an Amorite and your mother a Hittite. At
birth, on the day you were born, there was no one to cut
your umbilical cord or wash you in water to clean you,
or rub you with salt, or wrap you in swaddling clothes.
No one looked at you with kindness enough to do any of
these things out of pity for you. You were dumped in the
open fields in your own filth on the day of your birth. I
spotted you kicking on the ground as I passed by, and
I said to you, lying there in your blood: "Live!" And I
made you grow like the grass of the fields.

Ezekiel 16, 3–6

My mother was a Hittite and my father an Amorite.
My foster uncle was an albatross
and his brother-in-law ran a gambling joint in Altoona.
My cousins were stockbrokers in Scottsdale before the crash.
I was sold to strangers for a bag of wheat
and wandered the roads and the mountain passes
like a dark wind, touching and picking up
whatever came into my hands. I will stay alone many days
until I meet up once more with those men I knew in my youth:
men from Syracuse, men from Toledo,
men from Odessa and Scranton and New Alexandria,
and all those men from Assyria. They will assail me
and pinch my nipples, and pull up my skirt,
and make me pure with suffering.

My mother was a prophet and a priestess of suffering.
She walked the hospital corridors in her white robe
wringing the bones of her hands. My half-sister was a mudfish,
whispering warnings in the reeds of the marsh.
My mother was a whore, a midget, a human sacrifice,
and a candle guttering at the top of a stair. My father
came from another world that called him back,
and swallowed him like Saturn, like time,
like a world without oxygen, or a slow disease.
He was imprisoned in a tree by a sorceress
one hundred years; he rode with an army on black horses
that pounded the earth and raised dust in the mouths of settlers,
and when he died his papers were taken away and burned.
He then was drowned at sea.

My grandmother lived to ninety-seven years
through cunning and fornication,
but never came to visit or to claim me.
I was found beneath a tree by a herd of wildebeests
who fed me on salt water and tears of the dead.
I endured innumerable blows inflicted by hypocrites.
I lay cast out on the ground. No one
pitied me or looked on me with kindness.
A woman bore me and consented to have me killed.
I believe I have a human soul.
My name is Sorrow. I fell into the earth like a seed
and grew like the grass of the fields
and I am alive today by no one's grace or will.

Delinquent

Odd that the office would be so bright, painted in warm
shades of butter and honey, while outside the light

slammed down on fenders and on concrete posts and frozen
snowfields glazed with melt. This lockdown they call spring.

I had, God knows, no love for the grackles
mobbing the edges of the parking lot. The ice had melted

at the edges of the asphalt, and the frozen earth appeared to yield
some crumbs of seed or grass or insect carapace, yet I could not

stop watching them shoulder each other and threaten, with their
street-punk strut, bickering over privilege to pick at the hard ground.

In winter everything is winter and some must die, I thought.
I slouched in the blue eggshell chair, pulling at a thread

unraveling on my jeans and would not look up; sun hit my eyes
as voices hammered talk of consequences. All that was desired

lay frozen at my feet, lay on the other side of the wall.
I would fly through the window, scattering daggers of glass.

I would disappear in flame, leave only a shape of char.
When the world is your enemy, and speech an invitation

to open season on your body: slapped for a word, arrested for a sneer,
even silence a gesture interpreted by double agents of the mind,

give nothing away. Lock down. Hunch forward. Erase your face.
When they take you, as they will take you, away to where

they are going to take you, you'll be wound so tight you'll bounce;
you'll make a rattling noise on the ground, and whatever they break

in you, or break out of you will drag along behind, banging
and scraping, giving off long shrieks, obnoxious to their ears.

Feng Shui for Wartime

> The qi that rides the wind stops at the boundary of water.
>
> *Zangshu; The Book of Burial*
> *Han dynasty*

Wherever I turn, there is something ahead of me.
Yes, at every step a barrier.
No place is clear of claim,
so that what I pick up I cannot put down,
nor can I find what is lost, even in a single day.

The rigor of the world, its fire.
Bring kindness to yourself in every moment.
Bring kindness to the boxes, the dirty pots,
the barriers. Bring fire to my soul, o night;
the lights will come on again and find us
no better off and no less lost, for all our searching.

Suddenly the rush of engines ceases
—let the image clear—
so one's imagination pauses, settling in the plain
quiet of the countryside, the delta, Tigris
and Euphrates where cities lit by fire murmured
under moon's descending triangle, black sky, ages

before Abraham, or Alexander, the faint
wailing of ancient prayer,
the herds flowing softly across the plain.
Here I argued with a fellow citizen over the covered
storage bin on wheels given away at the dump,
lost the skirmish, took a colander and a book on
radical theology instead, justice for the poor,
while at home objects multiplied
like a scene from a horror film where ants
swarm to devour a peaceful settlement.

Red cashmere gloves with holes
in the fingertips, one could embroider flowers there,
two soccer balls, three picture frames, four hundred
DVDs, another chardonnay, and buffalo
chicken wings . . . damp towels . . . one turkey carcass
desiccating in the fridge
photos prohibited of the coffins

shipped to there and back the saddest cargo, patient, out of
time, create impediment to public confidence.

Just as a mirror can erase an entrance,
throwing you into the former world, bending time back,
just so the patrol meets a barrier,
shoes flung up, and broken glass and barrels,
rubble of brick—Clear! Clear!—the entrance is the exit,
no one moves in or out, we all
stay where we are. Refugee, you well remember
how to run, now stand as time runs through you.

Bring with you kindness and compassion
on approaching the great cubicle where pasts are stored

gas grills

        fox wraps wedding

                    portraits

artificial Christmas

        trees their unwound limbs writhing over
        grandmother's etagére: one

kayak fondue pot

           dog

              kennel foot spa decayed

electronic equipment crib
               gas dryer we have stored up treasure on this earth

and stood upon this hoard surmounting

               to defend at any cost whatever, yet

if the dead appeared to us restored, came forward
wearing their original faces,
sorting through cast-off clothing to cover their wounds,

who would not give them back the world, croon over
their beloved limbs and eyes and shyly stroke
their heads and hands and breathe their scent,
to bless with prayer what is burned
and scarred and made bitter,
the parts of the self hanging useless or bound, to treasure
at last the one, reparable body, for once comprehend
the numbered hairs of your head.

Meds

By the rivers of Babylon . . .
Psalm 137

1.

Living from pill to pill, from bed to couch,
what doesn't kill me only makes me dizzy.
Pain dissolves like chalk in water,
grit on the bottom of the glass.

Waiting takes forever,
throbs to the soles of my feet, *Bella noche* . . .

Hives as large as mice hump up under my skin
("no more barbiturates for you, Cynthia!")
—itch, stretch, I don't fit my flesh—
sting, tingle, prick, the sorcerer's threat.

There's a knife stabbed through my left eye.
My right foot is made of elephant hide
and weighs in at roughly one cartload of potatoes.
Oxygen twenty-four hours; I'm swelled with steroids,

prednisone buzz in the brain: a motel room
with sixteen foreign workers sleeping in shifts,
playing reggae at three a.m.

2.

Oh I love my white pill
that makes the black fist of pain unclench,
unspasming the nerves. I float,
released to darkness visible,
worlds dissolving.

And the yellow pill, bitter on my tongue,
that wakes me at 2 a.m.
writing out plans in Arabic
to organize an expedition to the Pole.
Drug of hubris searing my eyes,
my scrawl unreadable in daylight: foil my enemies.

Bitter taste of fugue,
my hand shakes: some foreign being in my brain giving orders.
You must You must You will.

Later, the pungent brown liquor
shoots the dark with threads of gold behind my eyes.
One flash as the mind goes out.

3.

I must elude pain
                              float past clarity
pain in the brain
                              slammed down like a housefly.

It's a big dodge.

Fly on a stovetop
                              sizzle and ash pop.

This is illusion,
                              mental confusion

                              born in the synapse.
What can be undone
                              down to the last gasp.
It's a hodgepodge.

If you kill pain

        you will become pain;

pain does not feel pain,

        no nerves in the brain.

It's a mind-fuck.

It's just your bad luck.

        A torpor sealed my brain
        I felt no humans near
        it seemed to me I could not feel
        or touch or see or hear.

I don't know who I am

        without my medicine.

My skin will crawl with bugs

        if I don't get my drugs.

My brain's a maelstrom,

        singing a sad song.

Reality is so cruel.

Prednisone oh prednisone
so fast my mind racing, never tasting
rest.

Razzle-dazzle razz

Fist bitch piss stitch witch . . .

        (only wait, the fit will pass.)

fast, gash, lash, splash—QUIT!

(I saw a werewolf in a white suit, walking
past the tables at the Full Moon Café.
Floppy bow tie, big furry hands.)

Percodan, Percocet, let you go, let you rest.
When the grip lets you go and you float like a note
on the flow, there's your life, there's no worry—
(yeah, it's funky how the night moves.)

Barbiturate babykins, narcotic slut,
black oil of opiate. Chatty Cathy, dirty brat,
bed-wetter, nasty pants.

Painkiller, painkiller, I have a new friend,
better than my old friend,
plugging holes in the brain:
Sigmund Freud, Sigmund Freud, Sigmund Freud, Cocaine!

I want a soft landing; let me float.
Once the seizure lifted me and threw me down.
I did not like it. I did not like lying there
on the floor looking up
through air like green water.

4.

And there is one so dark, a ghost,
it passes through the mesh of thought
without tearing a strand, whispering
destinies perceived true, pronouncing
sentences of death.

5.

A cloud, the absence of a noun, no name,
roaring far away in the summer

dark like a train, or a giant fan, or a highway that never stops.
The mind explodes in the dark of space,
unnursed by atmospheres,
as air raid sirens scream for blood
and I am only nerves, strung on constellations,
meridians and vectors quivering. A red and yellow
capsule invades the chemistry of thought; cathode rays blast
from the television screen and signals pass deep into space
until the stars are singing "Rosalita." You
will not remember this night.

Heavenly Bodies

This bitter morning in late winter
wind screamed around the house at dawn.
The strong sunlight withdrew
into the space between bodies.
We were still alive then, grieving.
Skid marks off the road. Snow blown from the peaks.
Driving to town to refill a prescription.

Gher the Hound

I woke in bloody sheets, the bandages undone,
the body's dream of pain unwound;
the torn flesh gapes, and yellow curds of fat
uprisen from the maw swell pale. Sweet fat
that makes the curve of arm round lovely,
that forms the turn of calf and lush of thigh.
Now blood runs red as blessing, cleans the wounds.

what flows away

I was walking in the high meadow,
parting waves of insects in wild grass. The voice said
lie down here
and be done with wandering.

My thoughts were philandering like bees.
I was transparent, safe as a maiden in the garden.
No maiden is safe in the garden.
The animal came upon me and I fought,
and beat at its head and neck, went for its eyes,
as red as if his shot out eyes bled bright
and blood exploded in his skull.
Claws ripped my arms
and nerves shot up like flames on a screen.

Dog's breath on my face, sick with my own
blood on his tongue, I fought. I held.
So once we owned dominion.

And yes, the fruit turns into a bird
and flies away.
The flower becomes a bee.
I am a woman, and I would not be
meat for the dead.
Lie down here and be done with wandering
for the kingdom is at hand.

The Elderberries

I picked the elderberries because I was poor
and an orphan, and falsely accused.
I picked the purple elderberries belonging to that woman
who watched me with suspicion, and recorded all my crimes.

My crime that day was theft.
Theft, and hunger, and ingratitude.
I picked the purple berries and ate them and licked
the stain of them from my hands, and the seeds,

and ate the little leaves that stuck to my fingers
and sucked at the collar of my dress where juices
ran down and left a dark stain on the cotton.
A drop of elderberry fell through the leaves
onto the back of a box turtle
who crawled away, bearing that testimony.

I ran and hid behind the tool and die factory
where men were honing molds in the whining spasms
of a steel saw. The sound hurt my ears.
I raised my arms to cover them
and saw my hands cut off, a dark stain
pumping methodically from my wrists,
spilled on to the ground.

She would have no use for me now.
And as I was poor and an orphan,
must I then be sacrificed?
I pressed my wrists together, cut to cut
to staunch the blood, to stay the surge,
the flux that would have emptied out my heart.

I gave up my arms like vines to this fusion;
I tied myself into a knot, a liana rooted to myself.
I gave up reaching,
became the one who could not claim or hold.
I was that determined to live.

The Judgment

Butternuts are dropping from the branches
the wind is thrashing this dead November.
Sky under my window white, empty

down to the ground, sky at the root,
sky in the clenching grasses, raining
dark green butternuts into the earth.

On the green landing, at the turn of the stair,
forbidden to come down, I make day
at the window. Hidden inside the drapes,

their swelling folds, their oak leaf pattern
like open hands with veins and small creases,
self-shrouded, I watch wind flay the trees.

Her palm raised to strike. Do not come down
again today, or let me see you. Do not cross
my sight, she said, to save me

from punishment, to keep herself
from hurting me. Mad child that I was,
did I want to make her hurt me?

The tree is wildly drumming its branches,
like something trying to get free of itself.
Like an error to be shaken off. My arm hurts,

the burned patch reddens. Leaned against
the window's chill, the raw flesh shines.
She screamed and spun in fury; boiling

water splashed over the pan, splattering
down—my fault, my error in surprising her.
Again my error, irrevocable . . .

The wind is tearing down the butternuts;
they pound the earth like someone kicking
at a door. Some split open when they hit,

the ridged seed hard and black inside,
the oily flesh ripped loose. They fall
into the earth and sink under the leaves.

The print of her fingers on my cheek:
a scald. Damn you! Damn you! she cried,
and I felt the air ignite. I want to go

and hide under the tangled grass,
and shrivel to a seed as hard as wood, to let
the hurt flesh wither and fall from my bones.

I want to be flung down by the wind, to lie
on the wet ground under leaves and sink
into the earth and find that deepest hell.

Dry Heart

God, why did you give me such a dry heart?
I think it must have been to help me live
in that house where the heart must be wrung,
in those years when I had to listen to everyone.
A dry heart taking nothing in.

I learned to say that I belonged to nothing.
But now I'm old; the people who hurt me are gone,
gone into the dark, and you have forgiven them—
that's right, I know, I knew you would forgive them,
but my heart you have not redeemed.

God, I have no heart. Why did you take my heart?
My heart that held its sorrow like baked earth,
my dry heart that refused to break or fail,
that waited out the seasons, patient, taking only
a little air. This muscle struggling inside me now,

thrashing the bone cage, is not my real heart.
It is an animal choking at the end of a rope,
a bird that batters its wings against stone,
and falls, and returns. Something wild and fierce,
desperate, and damned.

Whole House Gone to Hell

The mother who will not come down from her bed.
Television flickering across channels at odd hours:
the late movie, the news show at dawn, the all-night

mystery station. Milk gone sour in the refrigerator,
the daughter stumbling out of the backseat of a car,
hair in her eyes, her skirt wrinkled up at her hips.

The son sneaking out of the house to close a deal.
No one talks on the phone without shutting the door.
The rooms smell of smoke, yellow rot of nicotine.

The phlegmy cough. The father sunk in his chair,
growing hair from his arms and his hands.
The police, the ambulance, the pizza delivery.

The stretcher just clearing the turn of the stair.
Doctors' phone numbers taped to the refrigerator.
People begin to address each other obliquely,

directing pointed remarks to the dog.
Blood spattered behind the sink not washed away.
Parents meet children in the kitchen at 2 a.m.

and neither asks what the other is doing, and no
conversation is begun. Pills dropped on the carpet,
pink and blue among knots of lint behind the dresser.

The gun in the box on the floor of the closet, biding
its time. The knife in the drawer beside the stove,
biding its time. The cars in the garage asleep

with their eyes open, biding their time. Their engines
ticking. Smell of coffee burned on the stove,
someone coughing behind a door. The clock's red light

blinking beside the bed. Seconal, Nembutal,
Amytal, Percodan, Demerol, Valium, Thorazine.
Time is extinct and the moment is always.

Sleep gapes and opens like a fish's mouth,
but no one sleeps. A man is kicking trashcans
down a driveway, howling against their clang and peal.

It is 1967, late in the empire of America.
Years pass, and it is always this time. We wait, listening
for the silence after things stop falling.

Wake

Wake her at midnight—will she wake?
The damp in her hair, her wince and wild recoil,
her eyes rolled back against electric glare, the shock
of air. The sheet pulled back provokes a sudden chill,
revives the shrouded sleeper, lying there.

She, half-covered, barely breathing, lies
intact and cold, beyond you now. She will not, she
can not, you must not, touch, rouse—
oh wake her and save her at midnight, beloved,
risen to walk the hallway, lurch and drag, her face

crease-stitched with sleep, her eyes' light guttering.
She jerks her bird head to the side, spits rage,
comes toward you sliding one hand down the wall.

Again the stale breath, the terrible thirst.
Claim her then, wanton, ancient and wild,
her face so white and drawn. Now she sees you,
she screams: something in Assyrian, a curse.

Bride of the Barbiturate

She could do what she wanted,

cave them in her hands, hide

them, hoard them, make them

disappear. Dice. Stones. Little bones.

She could say what the doctor ordered,

and how many were left in the bottle

before she started swallowing one

after another—how many tonight

he doesn't know—his mind's

too slow, he cannot gauge,

she's gone beyond him,

skimmed his gaze, now falling

down through dream, she's floated,

riding wafts of air; he takes

her hand, limp tulip drooping

in his grasp, her jaw hung slack,

her eyes flat glass. Now she

will not refuse, he smoothes

her hair, no protest there.

He listens at her breast, the slow

heart strong, her breathing

soft, that languor nothing

will deny.

Recovery Room

in hospital light her hands tied down she kept
ripping the tube from her throat the IV she
fought gagging up the pills blood on her mouth

she bit her tongue fighting the hose shrieking why
have they seized her now away from that cool
darkness gone under to hear her heart gun and

flood to shine a beam into her eyes ghost
light glaring back through empty pupils have you never
seen the dead wakened cursing this world loathe to

return who ripped her from dark earth who brought
her here fighting red with fury whose act whose
need and fear signed orders dialed for help and

brought her to this wake her oh wake her
and walk her back to us let the dead
sleep let them rot as they are liable let

them rise in their invisible bodies before God he
walks the hallway glare too bright for night-spent eyes
his face grey hands steady carrying clothes from home

Monica

She came down the hill,
cutting through the backyards
of lighted houses, a bag of apples
clutched in her arms, her sneakers
slipping on the wet grass.
The dusk was smoke-colored,
purple chrysanthemums and yellow
leaves subsiding to drab,
and already the moon rising
full and transparent, behind the brick houses.
She wanted to give me the apples:
"We have so many!" and I took them
and stood talking, wondering what to do.
I was home before midterms,
my bag heavy with books, ponderous
chronicles of the wreck of the century:
Warsaw, Paris, St. Petersburg, Berlin. . . .
Her daughter, who had been my friend,
and the baby, and Jerry, were living in the next town.
Jerry was going to school nights.
I should go see them—she said it
without reproach, wanting to make things right.
I had three days
and I would go back on the bus. I said yes,
thinking no, and stood there
holding the brown paper sack on my hip,
bulging, bumpy, hard. The apples
smelled only cold, the way the air smelled,
and the night coming up behind us,
empty and hard, cold water and rock.
She turned and went back up the hill.
Back inside, I set the apples on the table,
letting them spill out, and I sat down
with my books under a bright overhead light

as night closed over the house
where I sat and read, not comprehending
the wreck of that century, ending,
helpless before all I did not know.
Turning pages in the kitchen,
the empty house creaked and settled
as the scent of the apples lifted, warming,
their skins glaring deep red
with brown patches and spots of yellow,
the cider tang wakening in them
as I read, unaware of the night closing
over me, the year ending, stars
pulling back into deep space
and the planet tipping toward dark,
the earth's last gifts.

II

Shot Up in the Sexual Revolution:
The True Adventures of Suzy Creamcheese

"So, why don't you sleep with girls?"
"I'm not really attracted to girls."
"Are you telling me you were really
attracted to every man you slept with?"
Conversation with a friend

1.

After twenty I stopped counting,
not like my friend Beverly, who sewed
an embroidered satin star on her bell-bottoms
for every new guy she fucked.
She had them running down both legs
and around the billowing hem,
and was starting up the inseam
when the jeans gave out in the wash.

It was a boys' game anyway, those years
of our extended homage to the penis:
the guitar playing the penis, drums saluting it,
cock rock, Molotov cocktail, the motorcycle
gripped between the thighs, and I went down,
we all went down, in the old cultural disaster
of idol worship—a thousand-year bender.
Only this time it was the adolescent member,
oiled and laved, thrust forward arcing,
thin with ache, all tight flesh poked upward,
claiming its own. How it came and went,
penetrating but never settling down,
and how often we were caused to admire it:
hairless sweet warrior, raider against the State.

But I have this sweet pink flower
here between my legs—I put my hand down and touch it,
still soft and wet, and many-folded, endlessly opening,
hiding, seeking, hidden and sought,
but never very much admired or even smiled on
in those years, never served much less sung to.
Not a garden then but a citadel,
a wall to be breached, a new land claimed,
but linger there? No, I would say
there was an overall lack of appreciation,

though breasts were well respected, slopping loose
under T-shirts like little animals,
and I would feel my nipples brush the cotton
with pleasure, see them regarded also with pleasure.
Still, sex then was a taking, like spoils of war, a victory
over all those straight fucks back home, marooned
in the dismal suburbs that birthed us squalling and red
and watched us flee in ungrateful cars down night highways.

And God knows it felt good those nights.
I was ready, it was ready, to open and answer the call.
And take me down and roll me over, yes, and give
it to me—but why all this riding away afterward?

Where was everyone going
and why didn't I get to ride along? Who knew at first
nothing had changed, just wanting the thrust and tug
and slam up against the headboard, I should say so,
but left still wanting more, wanting to leap
out of centuries' shame and be something new,
not this old consolation of women for the powerless,
some kind of cosmic door prize awarded
just for showing up with a dick,
some proof to themselves these boys were men.

"You're good," he said. Hell, I wasn't taking a typing test,
I was fighting to live in a dying world.
I was throwing myself away, an offering to wildest space,
surrender to the mind's dissolve, the body's electric light,
nerve endings firing like exploding stars.
"You're good," they all said:
you'd think somebody was doing a survey.
Girls say yes to boys who say no, and then
your professor asks if you're wearing underwear,
when you meet for your conference on the poetry of Yeats.

Crossing the border after midnight in a borrowed car
after a visit to the after-hours doctor's office in Sarnia.
Nodding out in the back seat, pills wearing off.
He was a legend among undergraduates:
cheap and reliable, always on call,
until a month later the headlines screamed
"Abortion Doc!" when a girl died in his office
and he dragged her down to the river
and dumped her body in the underbrush.

2.

So you move in with the guy: an old farmhouse
with a couch on the porch, half a dozen cars in the yard.
Days come and go; people come and go.
Soon wearing those handmade-in-Guatemala cotton dresses
that ravel at the hem and bunch up around your waist.

I slid back in history, canning tomatoes and stirring
the lentil soup my ancestors spurned two hundred years ago
when they sailed for America and a better life.

Cast me back in time, tents and wood fires,
teepees and yurts, and squatting by a bush to pee.
Passing infections, hepatitis and crabs,
not getting hung up on jealousy or possession.
Old lady, old man, welfare babies named Sky and Isis:
"Hippies treat their women like squaws."

Smoking homegrown weed, drying Mexican mushrooms:
those were the brown years, a study in earth tones,
granola, brown rice, nuts and seeds,
brown bread and brown acid, hash brownies,
grass brownies, carob cake and macramé.
The more work anything took the more authentic it seemed,
while we listened to industrial rock and roll
and roamed the highways in German microbuses
carrying our pink plastic dial packs
of state-of-the-art contraceptives.
No latex, no calendar, never miss a day.

And I hate to say it but the men were regressing
at warp speed into permanent adolescence of air guitar
and arcane secrets of how to roll a joint so tight
it would burn forever, and letting their brain cells
simmer, or maybe they just weren't getting enough protein
or fresh air, inhaling incense and wood smoke between tokes.

But who would return
to the ranch house on the green mowed cul-de-sac,
those comfortable concentration camps
furnished with harvest gold appliances and shag carpeting?
And the ones left behind—
wage slaves stoned on barbiturates and television,
all sleeping with the neighbors anyway
and wearing those drip-dry perma press shirts
with the little pockets? It seemed there was no way back
and the world was alight with new dangers,
so surely this was not the end of the adventure . . .

3.

So you move in with the guy and get political.
Captive since Troy, I learned to run a mimeograph
and make stacks of sandwiches, toting gallons
of coffee laced with benzedrine to fuel all-night meetings
to bring down the state. I learned to keep my mouth
shut and my legs open. "The correct position for women
in the movement is horizontal." IUD bleeding and cramps.
Blood clots and cancer scare from the pill.
Come home on your Dalkon shield. Cocaine,
acid, and crystal meth: ball all night
and blow your mind with revolutionary theory.
"Put your body on the line." We meant it.
The world was changing out there in the streets,
where the masses would rise up to claim their own,
and we'd be with them, waving and shouting:
All war is murder— All property is theft!

The cities were burning
and the streets were more dangerous than ever
but no one would walk you home. Weren't we
liberated? Upholding class solidarity: it was
a compliment if a man yelled at you on the street
or even grabbed your ass, and if he followed you home
and you couldn't get rid of him, well,
that didn't even have a name. It wasn't rape
unless he had a gun and you fought for your life.

I only wanted to walk with my eyes up
ready to meet every gaze, wanting the streets to be mine
as they were anyone's. But it was still a boys' game.
"The movement hangs together on the head of a penis."
Women were learning massage or singing backup
or waiting tables to keep him in art school
and out of the army—it was no time to think of ourselves
with the war needing ending and the cities in flames.

4.

So, I slept with my lovers, I slept with my friends,
my lovers' friends and my friends' lovers,
friends of friends and so on. I slept with my dealer
and my dealer's dealer, just to be sure.
I slept with some men I barely knew
to prove I was open-minded, or to avoid an argument,
and I slept with some men I didn't like
just to be nice, or, well, to avoid an argument.
You might say I had an open door policy.

I took it three ways, I took it sideways:
"thousands of men and a few hundred women."
Hum jobs, tie me up, half and half, and fuck the dog.
I took it in the ass, in my mouth, between my thighs
and way up inside from any angle. Yet what I loved most
was hard dancing to loud music: that beat through the floor,
and bodies swaying, sweating, the tension building,
and getting just to the edge of it, in a room, in a woods,
down a hallway wedged inside a bathroom stall, falling
down fast, or leaning back brace yourself
on the wall, diving into it like stepping on a mine—just
blowing yourself up, all the while holding on
to some sweating panting guy also blowing himself up—
just kick out the door hard mindless sex—I wanted it
as much as the next guy, the next high priestess of come,
and it was ours and all new and fine, and would never end,

until one day love comes roiling up like swamp gas
fermented for years in the collective unconscious
of old songs and bad movies, a distant memory wakening.
His thumbs in his belt loops, his crooked smile
and dark moods, and you think this one is a god
or an avatar of destiny, and you're nothing unless
he loves you too, and now everything is changed
and you let your life go, like a bad gene or a slow virus.
You've bought the gypsy's curse, the heroine's undoing,
that fatal weakness inscribed in a hundred novels
you read as a girl in your sweet gabled bedroom
while you were waiting for your life to happen.

5.

So you move in with the guy, and he's writing a book;
he's having a vision, he's painting a fresco.
You become shadow artist, muse to his legend,
all smoke dreams and not bumming his high.
Nights he spends brooding, you wait up, ready
to fry an egg at midnight to comfort his despair.

Or, and why not,
pick up and move to another city,
tramp around Greece or Spain.
Maybe he gets a gig and you go with him to the coast
and you're back waiting tables to make the rent,
and he's writing rock and roll reviews,
with a backstage pass and too much time on his hands.

Until you come home early from work one night,
smelling of fries, and he's got some girl in the bed
she's maybe sixteen, they're watching cartoons all naked
and eating Chinese; they just smile up at you
and who would blame you then
if you picked up that little TV from the cart
and threw it into the wall so it sparks and flashes down
all over them and they're scrambling out from under
all white legs and buttery butts
and you just stand there looking on calm, but you don't,
that's too retrograde old school possession, too many
middle class expectations so you don't freak out you're very
cool, but you think of it later then you break down and cry
and say you really love him and you're just
a girl again, hating yourself, and nothing has changed.

6.

So you leave the city, plan to make it on your own,
or, why not, hit the road, hitch to the coast,
grab the overnight charter to Brussels by way of Iceland,
sleep on the fly. Sleep on the subway, sleep in the park,
get beat up cutting through the cemetery at midnight,
discover the dubious protection of the law.
Learn to watch what's ahead of you and what's behind you;
don't walk too slow; try to look like you have someplace to go.
Even a woman lingering by a store window
may be mistaken for a prostitute.

And girls turn up by the road, rolled in leaves and dirt,
and the ones taken in by lunatics on communes devoted to Armageddon,
whose leaders leap up in rage during their murder trials to shriek:
"My thoughts light fires in your cities!"

7.

I tell you, I ran away once and I'm still running.
The collective, the commune, the family, the movement . . .
The rundown farmhouse with sixteen scraggly hippies
and strangers sleeping over was not, for me, a hearth to defend.
Remember the bathtub with everybody's hair in the drain.
Stir the soybeans, or fuck it, let them burn. Get up
off the dusty floor cushion of your anarchist manifesto
and the Book of the Dead, and let a single brain cell fire
long enough to complete a sentence, or at least
bring in the mail. Strum on your guitar, but don't talk to me
about world justice. There's work to be done, and when I
raise your consciousness this time, something's gonna burn.

Oh, I admit you were beautiful to me, each dog-faced man-child,
steaming with revolution, and the absolute confidence
of sexual privilege, each of you who opened my jeans
with a smile of having arrived at your inheritance, having
touched land in the new world, nothing in your way,
and all that fruit for the taking.

Yes, and wasn't it all tight pink flesh,
your cock standing up so hard it nudged your navel;
my breasts pointing upward with a little smile:
not a sag or a fold or a sad daddy's greying nest
of chest hair could touch us. We were smooth,
we could have been comrades, bending it together,
those years when I wore an army jacket
and you had your hair in a braid.

Now I'm choked on analysis, bored respectable.
I'm too old for the drugs, my body can't take it,
though I'll never really get clean. I've got more
prescriptions than Elvis. I'm hallucinating
on hormones, zoned out on Xanax; I get dizzy
when the blood thinners kick in. And I'd like to say

I still have my memories, but my memories are disintegrating
faster than tissue paper in a wet drain. I'm too proud
to go hunting for rock and roll on the classics band
and as for sex, well, that should still be a possibility
though I am pretty pissed off and hope is fading, yet
the feeling keeps coming back—it doesn't ever go away.
It's still warm and sweet down there, that cunt
framed with damp and curly hair, and I think maybe
it could go on forever: rebel without a pause,
the hormone years, It could be possible

if anything were possible
that didn't make me feel caught in a time warp,
with that little girl gaze and pale hope everlasting,
knowing how sex is in me forever, its electric connections
fused on the body's own currents, and I keep going down
to that place where thought stops and the power rises,
that old outlaw in me singing "Desperado"
in the dark with gravel in my voice, still wanting more.

8.

Adam, the serpent gave me the apple and I did eat.
You took it from my hand, my dear. We stand here naked,
forsaken; the wind blows through the leaves.
There's nobody else around. Rise,
make me shy again, soft as a feathered thing,
glad to raise my mouth to your mouth, to open
my lips to your lips. Try it once more,
till we get it right. Try it twice. I never was counting.
We were beautiful. Nothing is forgiven.
Do you like it this way then? Take me down.
Touch me there. Hold me,
kiss me. Yes, kick out the jams;
we are stardust, carbon;
we are garden. Foxy lady, Ooh,
Baby, Baby . . .

III

Coyote

Do not invite him lightly to your bed.
This is a man of persistence and great sloth.
Sweet leaves brought slowly to the mouth; the branch
Bent down, low constant sounds, a hum along

The neck, the nape, the nipple—his tongue's long,
Ostensible kisses. This is a man
Who wants to rearrange your furniture, to devour
Your resumé. Do not ask him to see you across

The river. The glow of your cheek on the pillowcase,
Creased hieroglyphic of time the skin recalls,
Invites discovery. A branch snaps underfoot,
The leaves speak backwards: forget . . .

Your day job. Your night school. Your green canopy.
By morning your passport wears another name.

Some Testimony of Witnesses

I went down to where the object had
been. I noticed the brush was burning.
I noticed smoldering bushes but they
felt cold to the touch.

Missing Time, *Budd Hopkins*

1.

Blue light in the pine barrens, a sudden rush of cold.

Uneasiness along a certain stretch of road.

I saw beings with icy red energy,

grey-white beings with oblong heads and no eyes.

A blue disk hung in the sky; it seemed alive;

it seemed alive with consciousness.

I walked out of the woods. They were looking for me.

I had blood on my shirt. The only thing I can remember

is that I saw a beautiful deer in the woods.

It was almost like a mystical deer.

2.

Summer night, northern summer, the kitchen door open
to let in the breeze. Nothing to fear there in the night.
The light was worldly, yellow cigarette smoke,
white mugs with coffee. Aunts and uncles
leaned their elbows on the kitchen table.
People walked from one room to another
and if, at the end of a field,
the veil between worlds lifted
like a light, like shiny silver, like a woman in pain,
there was no one to see it
except the lost and brokenhearted people
wandering off the roads, one traveler
knocked to the ground by a great wind
and a whirring like locusts, who lay there
on the soft grass of the hillside,
and woke and went on,
knowing he would not be believed.

Down the road the drive-in's
huge screen showed a terrible lizard
destroying a city, his great claw
toppling buildings: the people were incidental,
falling silently down the sky.

The cat cries at the screen for ghosts.
Through the dark our eyes can't penetrate
he senses the strange, the distant eye
probing us, here in this lonely place.
Night transforms reason:
When all we have refused or forgotten
returns seeking us, will we turn away?
How can we know they mean us no harm?

3.

Mary glows on the bureau, her red-gored heart pulsing,
as Patty tells me of a room in the college museum
where there are nine jars on a shelf.
Floating there in some liquid, she says:
"the bodies of babies who were never born."
One month to nine, the last one crowded up
against the glass, its flesh pressed into it,
flattening. "They have their eyes open;
they are all curled up," she says.
(I have seen them: it is as she said;
their skin is yellowish, like ancient teeth.)

Summer thunder far off, heat lightning, no rain.
A wave of sickness overwhelms me,
as if I were approaching some final peak
where I have vowed to leap. Never born,
half-made creatures displayed on a shelf.
If you moved them they would bob a little,
making ripples in formaldehyde, perhaps a limb
floating loose, a hand opening.

They hang unclaimed in the empty room at night.
These aliens with the faces of Hiroshima.

Something is out there. A man and a woman
naked, slipped into each other; she
in his arms disappeared in him, opened; he pushed
up into her opening, and my life began, that
shudder rippling time, things we never speak of.
Star stuff stirred up, their undoing.

In the night come thoughts, and images of thoughts.

4.

Ancient instructions for meeting the jinns contained warnings and special marks by which to recognize the well- or evil-intentioned ones. Some are demons or fallen angels, some merely uncontrolled thought forms, or human discarnates.

Characteristics of jinns:

1. In their normal state they are not visible to ordinary human sight.

2. They are, however, capable of materializing and appearing in the physical world, and can make themselves visible or invisible at will.

3. They can change shape and appear in any sort of guise, large or small.

4. They are able to appear in the guise of animals. (Owls, large spiders, and horses figure prominently.)

5. They are inveterate liars and deceivers, and delight in bamboozling and misleading mankind with all manner of nonsense.

6. They are addicted to the abduction and kidnapping of humans.

7. They delight in tempting humans into sexual intercourse.

8. The jinns are wont to snatch up humans and teleport or transport them almost instantly, setting them down again miles away.

5.

In the guise of animals: owls, large spiders, and horses.
In the guise of Chevrolets, headlights and fins, a steel beast
that spins and hovers, shine and glitter, speed and quick turns.
In the guise of burn victims with no eyelids
and holes for mouths, hairless and stiff.
In the guise of animals. In the guise of dark patches
on your palms and heels, around your navel, unexplained scars.
In the guise of amnesia and the fear of sleep.
The fear that says you are approaching some thought
you have been working toward for years, clearing a path
with your hands through thorns and brush, a clear thought
    that will change
everything. In the guise of the dead friend risen, not meeting
your eyes, and letting loose a swarm of wasps in the hallway.
In grief for our dead, and our sins against them.

In the guise of dwarfs with enormous heads bursting with
    intelligence.
In the guise of lemur-like creatures covered with hair and claws,
or monsters in armor like giant insects. In the guise of infants.
In the guise of animals.

6.

Events came to me. I didn't seek them out.

My life has always been one thing, one place. Things happened somewhere else. I knew your father, and your mother's sister. For years nothing changed.

The glass on my windshield is scratched, hazy. A dust storm out of nowhere, then those lights. Dust pitted the glass, choked the air. I stayed inside the car; it was terribly cold.

And then I woke. Everything was still. Hours had passed and I could not remember anything and my body was stiff and sore.

I don't know if the people I see here are the real people. They may all be pretending; they may be make-believe people, or replacements. I don't sleep at night. I sit at the kitchen table, waiting. It's as if something was half told to me and I'm afraid to hear the end, but I can't go on until I do.

When I dream I see shooting blue lights over the trees, grey oblong faces.

St. Michael, Archangel, defend us in battle. Be our protection against the wickedness and snares of the Devil. May God rebuke him, we humbly pray, and do thou, O Prince of the heavenly host, by the power of God, thrust into hell Satan and all evil spirits, who wander through the world, seeking the destruction of souls.

7.

I saw pinpoints of light in geese-like formations.

There was a blue-light body person. Beings.

They touched me. They implanted something in my abdomen.

They made a slit in my arm. It did not seem to bleed.

We have to stop talking now. I am not supposed to remember.

The examining table, where . . .

Fear. And a rush of cold. These weightless thoughts

Come at night. These owls quiet in the winter branches,

Grey as branches, still as winter trees. A mind brooding.

One witness remembered only

An odor of burned toast and lilacs . . .

The Hunting Camp

1.

Yesterday
out walking in the woods, discovered
black bear's butt hair on a tree.
Scratching her ass in pleasure, she,
waking hungry in hairy spring comes roaring
down the hill, and it is snowing.

2.

Heads of the dead
deer are hung on the wall,
up high, glass for eyes. Faces
of the dead founders glow
down behind glass above
the fieldstone fireplace, to bless
our meal of meat and wine.
Portraits in golden frames.
Velvet nostrils sprayed for mites,
and old, rare carpets.

3.

I'm going to sign my name
on a plaque and nail it
to the wall. I'm going
to sign my name on a plaque
and nail it to the wall.
I'm going to sign
my name. I'm going to know
where I am next time
if ever I find myself
back here again.

4.

Footprints pock the snow.
Red bulls-eye on a tree.
White markers every ten yards. Still,
I have gotten lost in the woods.

Pick up a stick if you hear the dogs
running. I'm pissing
in the snow, letting go
a hot stream, strong and gold.
Inside my body the world
is bright yellow. Trees
store sunlight in leaves.
I keep this light inside
myself against a darker day.

5.

I am so hungry, the owl
says with her wings,
and flies away, and eats.
I am so hungry,
the rat says, fleeing
the woodshed, and is picked
up and eaten, and so knows
the end of hunger.

I love you and I am hungry so
I will track you down and know
at once the end of love.

6.

I shot an arrow in the air.
It came to earth I do not care
where unless it pierced
the heart or brain or liver or gut
of the great beast I desire
to eat and wear the skin of on
my cold and fragile bones.
My flesh still winter white . . .

7.

I want to get very rich and famous
so everyone will want to fuck me.
I want to be famous so everyone
will want to fuck me. It's hard
to get famous for fucking, but it's easy
to get fucked when you're famous.

8.

Walking in woods is slow
in snow, in early spring. Listen:
turn your ear. A branch, a crunch
of frozen crust. Sometimes
they come too near.
A fed bear is a dead bear.
They like suet and birdseed
and also honey mustard barbecue.
I fed popcorn to a chipmunk
because his pointed, inquisitive gaze
flattered me. You cannot feed
a mouse to a snake.
The snake will help himself.

9.

Hawk feather on the path.
When desire leaves us we are like children.

10.

There is a mold that lives on
the food of human beings.
There are certain molds, and germs and fungi
and infestations of lice in the ears
and the nostrils of trophies,
and in the knotted threads
of the rare carpets
of the dead founders.

11.

The hunters are lost in the woods;
(hunters lost in the woods)
they fire their guns in the air
(fire their guns in the air)
and call and scare the deer.

But they each have their own thermos,
their oatmeal and raisin cookies,
and sandwiches wrapped in waxed paper.
So they just sit down and stare around,
lean back against a tree, and wait to be found.

Foundling

Renunciation . . . is a piercing virtue.

Emily Dickinson

But to be the one renounced
in name of virtue—that's a bad joke,
a taste in the mouth like last night's garlic.
Sweat it out. Comes the wound without the honor,
like the martyr soldier's horse.
Insult to fibers moral and connective.
Do I shame you? So I shame you.
Your secret's showing, not to be spoken.
Rumor in the blood refused: call me applecart
upsetter, homewrecker, closet skeleton;
the story is well known. The hills above this city
are scarred with infants' bones.

Dirt Cowboy Café

Heart, oh heart,
I sit here writing your name
on pieces of paper,
folded, hidden, misplaced . . .
found again.

There is the element of saying
and there is the element of making:
one needn't choose.
I am singing the dream out from the ice,
asking it to carry me
like a horse or a river, down and away.

This day, here in paned-glass sun:
the young waitress shaking out her apron
and retying it flat across her stomach—
a bit of vanity—her hair swept off her neck,
crash of a milk bottle
on the granite counter, cream
spread in a mild pool toward the rim,
and the roots of habit and longing
briefly seized by the mind.

So noisy here! The sound echoes
out of years, brought to this
showing forth, unrehearsed.
It seems we wake
and find ourselves repeating,
embodying the ancient gestures
by which we recognize
ourselves completed.

Not one of us could be born
and invent life—it must show through us—
the arm flung in the air, the coffee poured out,
and down the street, someone hurrying by,
head down against the wind.

And a man and a woman
come to an old grief,
carved in them, carved
into them
—the old way of water wearing rock—
by law, and the hatred
between them is equal
to the hope neither will release.

Each wants to be whole,
to embody all of time, when nothing
in this world is whole, and
this is by law.

When my father said bitterly
to my mother: *you have changed*,
he meant, without meaning to say,
how she had changed him. A man
holds his head down against the wind.
Yet the wind fills him
with the dust of temples,
the breath of the dead.

The dream of the light
inside the branches—
a gleam of wet, glimmer that is a bud,
the leaf within the bud.

The photographer comes inside
and closes the lens of his camera.
Then he is the lens. Then my eye
is the light. This
is the element of saying.
The young waitress flings a paper cup
behind her, into the trash can.
That is a saying. The cream swirled
into the coffee, the sugar
dissolving, disembodied,
and the body of the manager disappears,
swallowed into a doorway.

The element of making is slow,
uncertain as a temple,
a falling forward, stitching back,
like a stone wall, like the panes in an
arched window, like a repetition
chosen beyond necessity.

Yet somehow we have seen all this before—
the girl in the fur hat
speaking syrup into a phone;
the falseness of her charm
is an ancient imposter, familiar and
therefore true.
A door is opened and falls
closed. Suddenly at every table
someone looks down and is reading—
books, newspapers, calendars,
reading tea leaves, reading bones.

A woman in a periwinkle jacket: I am reading
her shoulders as the day introspects.
In dream the passive construction
and the past perfect tense prevail:
she was being pushed on a swing.
The woman with many television credits
gazes out the window, heavy with years,
forgetting herself, forgetting sorrow,
the false husband, the crippled child,
the old plots forgetting,

and it is suddenly lovely, as free as
something read or dreamed; the young
waitress with sun on her
face—her unblemished face—looks up,
from the middle of eternity, her desire
immaculate in the moment.

When a word is beautiful
above all others—*your name*—
when a woman appears as a bird of prey
and we turn away,
hoping not to be recognized—*oh heart!*—

when the light on the branches
flares in a window with no sky,
this is old story reading us, these are springs
from words laid down before
and ahead of us, and in the moment
we are making an answer.

Goldfinches in a Dull Light

for my mother

Snow in April.

And I will leave footprints
in the slow dawn
     and the deer will come, yearling fawn and doe,
     brown and warm, their gazes calm,

to the edge of the trees, wondering . . .
     what is this season, white and strange,

this snow falling, frail,
into waves of dark earth? I walked out
in the grass to see

the trail already dissolving. Melting,
the earth takes in
footprints like rain. We
vanish so easily . . .

1st fragment: the Nightgown Ballet.
Fragment 2: your little dog scratching the door.
Fragment 3: stain of shame . . .
     scrubbing, scrubbing the cloth.

And snow makes a maze of sky;
hemlocks high along the ridge
     wave dark arms,
     up and down, scarcely moving.

Snow, dust, ash born on air.
It snows into morning. The deer
are inside it now.

Fragment 4: Ambulance summoned.
Fragment 5: I don't remember.
Fragments 6 and 7: the Nightmare of Barbiturate.
Fragment 8: The one with the car and exile.

The purple tulip opened, snow swelling
its heart, bearing the cold flower,
the daffodil bent down.

And the goldfinches in dull light
bring their hunger to the frost-bit grass,
seek the dark meat of seed; the heart
beating, burning air,
will not abate. In the grass I see
a hundred villages,
and you are ash.

My Brother Is Moving to Hawaii

Now in the night there must be lizards, and bats with orange eyes,
a scent of ginger and perfume, and flowers dropping petals on bare earth.

Sweet air, the taste of conch, a pool with swaying lights below,
and here—a barbecue! Smoke and sugar, meat and salt:

the milk of coconut, and chlorine blue, so easy on the eyes.
Inhale once more the oldest dream of Europe, world that never knew

its own ennui, the vastness of its lust for luxury—the bite
of sugar on the tongue, sweet pang of slave-song sung to stars

—until teas from India, jewels and silks from China, gunpowder, gold,
tobacco, rum, seduced like opium, and sent the continent on

a buying spree. We all are masters now, and sons of kings.
This quest made manifest, to traffic gold and flesh, and sail us,

land us, after centuries, here. And here the world is blue,
the air like water lapping, water the color of tiles, these thorns

on the spray of meadow pandemic flowers hooked in my hair,
like particular desires. Comes now the bride of illusion,

bearing a platter of baked schoolteacher fish, garnished with snow tire
root vegetable puree, of which I eat, and pronounce myself free.

I'm here to forget about thirty bad years. Pass the bikini salt
and brown thigh dressing, subtle on the tongue. We have been dreary

too long, lingered in climates best suited for preserving dust.
Here paper rots. A blossom damp and crumbled on the ground.

I will not work today, or work tomorrow. I will taste mango
and papaya and roast pig. I will not sleep alone—the night

is full of moving bodies like my own. I have left my life,
my bills, my forms unfilled. I will not pay, or tell them where I am.

I have some hash, a pocketful of pills, this lizard is my friend,
my son has changed his name and gone away to school.

My former wives and current creditors can all go fuck themselves.
I like that I don't know the names of anything that grows here:

jasmine, tuberose, hibiscus. Words that speak forgetting. *Frangipani* . . .
I'm glad I shipped my truck so I have something to drive around in

under these whatever-you-call-them palms. Scent of blossoms
and sweet ocean breeze, the sound of my guitar plucked,

single notes like fruit falling, soft. Language of vowels,
caressing me: never two consonants together. This I know,

from my wahini: *Ukelele* means leaping flea. *Aloha* means love.
Haole is devil, or foreigner, white man. *Pupele* is crazy.

Cut Flowers

Though the cut flowers wilt
and the leaves wither, blanching
in the vase for days, still
they remind me of fields, the loveliness
of fading part by part, so many
changes, not sudden the cutting
down, not brutal but a way of
undoing. A fulfillment.
Merciful, you could say,
the cutting down and then
the slow undoing, which returns
forms to their beginning
as they go, petal by petal, and leaf
curling, how one shrivels
and falls. A blossom
that folds in on itself, remembering
the bud. Complete in its beginning.
As we say the flower is perfect,
and I feel my soul in danger
if I believe this because I am
a flower, no, a field of imperfections
and I may yet be cut down.
Be mercifully undone.
I'm sitting by the window and it is night;
I smell the cut grass, and gasoline
burning in cars that pass, and an insinuation
of skunk—these frighten me
because I cannot join them; they are not
sorrow or undoing, they are life fulfilling itself,
and I cannot settle my mind
from this ungainly sadness.
The window is open;
the flowers lean away from it, wilting.
A wish that I might be, not spared,

but taken back into this
night garden, made part of
something. This "I" a blossom
that opens and falls,
taken into a smell of cut grass,
whatever comes to me, for me,
across night, flown to this
single window, lit
from within by lamplight.

A faintest fragrance of fields
persists in these flowers, still lovely,
wilting without sorrow, without knowing loss.
And yet grief lives in the corners
and under our hair and nails, private
and untended against the world's machine.
It prevails, this grief,
wrapped in moderation, and making small
gestures toward what breaks
the heart. But everything breaks the heart!
It is here to break, only invented to be
the fist of blood that bursts in the fire.
Why I love the wilting
flowers and the greens rotting
in the yellowing water, not gently,
not gently at all, but like some dead animal
held in the hand. It is not
merciful, I was wrong
to say "merciful," that was wish only.
I have come to a place
here at the kitchen table where nothing
consoles me but these flowers
detonating silently by the window.

Somewhere a meadow strewn
with flowers untidy as stars, shimmers
in light. A meadow uncut, never turned.
I think I am talking about fear
and I know fear is only ignorance
of our true nature, mistaking
the loss of ourselves for an end
of being. The flowers stand up in the air
beside the window. They were not slain,
they were not rolled in heaps
into ditches to lie upon one another;
they stand up in the air beside the window,
translated, waning
as life wanes, in normal use, not in terror.
I am sitting by the window.
I am looking at the flowers.
The night air is cool and I breathe it
into every cell. Molecules of
darkness become me.

Notes

"Bastard's Song"

Some phrasing is inspired by or paraphrased from *The Three Christs of Ypsilanti,* by Milton Rokeach.

"Shot Up in the Sexual Revolution"

Suzy Creamcheese: fictional teenybopper from Salt Lake City, created by Frank Zappa and the Mothers of Invention. They portrayed her as sexually desirable but clueless and uptight.

"Girls say yes to boys who say no": war slogan, coined by Joan Baez.

"Hippies treat their women like squaws": Danny Rifkin's mother. Danny Rifkin was the road manager for the Grateful Dead.

Betty Friedan called the suburbs "comfortable concentration camps for women."

"The correct position for women in the movement is horizontal": Stokely Carmichael.

The Dalkon Shield was an intrauterine birth control device popular in the late 1960s and early '70s. It caused severe cramping and bleeding and was recalled in the wake of a class action suit after it led to scarring and infertility in thousands of women.

"Put your body on the line.": Mario Salvo, Berkeley Free Speech Movement.

"The movement hangs together on the head of a penis": Interestingly, Todd Gitlin attributes this quote to Tom Hayden in his memoir, and Tom Hayden attributes it to Gitlin.

When a reporter claimed that Janis Joplin was a lesbian, she said, "You go and tell that son of a bitch I've slept with thousands of men and a few hundred women."

"My thoughts light fires in your cities.": quote from Charles Manson at his trial.

"Some Testimony of Witnesses"

Some references to UFO sightings and abductions are inspired by, and in some cases paraphrased from, accounts by witnesses recorded in *Missing Time,* by Budd Hopkins; *Your Sixth Sense*, by Belleruth Naparste; and *Diary of an Abduction*, by Angela Thompson.

"These space guests are sometimes idealized figures along the lines of technological angels who are concerned for our welfare, sometimes dwarfs with enormous heads bursting with intelligence, sometimes lemur-like creatures covered with hair and equipped with claws, or dwarfish monsters clad in armour and looking like insects." *Flying Saucers*, C. G. Jung.

"Characteristics of Jinns" has appeared in different versions on numerous websites. The original version is attributed to Gordon Creighton, in *Flying Saucer Review*."

"Events came to me. I didn't seek them out": *Missing Time*, Budd Hopkins.

Other Books in the Crab Orchard Series in Poetry